Grasses of Nashville Township

m otis aavenüe

Compiled and produced by microdot media | Unalaska, AK 99692
A Matt Reinders Proprietary Business

Visit www.microdotbooks.com for more information.
Please address inquires to:

otis.aavenue@gmail.com

Subject: MicroDot Media & Grasses of Nashville Township

Library of Congress Cataloging-in-Publication Data

Library of Congress Control Number: 2011961380

ISBN-13: 978-0-9848553-0-8

1. poetry – young adult – adult
page count: 52

Manufactured in the United States of America

Written for friends and family in Nashville Township
and Faribault County, Minnesota.

CONTENTS

EXIT
102

Waiting for Letters to Deliver

On Rural Route 1
passed railroad signs
and a granite bed of rail timbers.
An old sidewalk
approaches the abandoned school.
The truant bell no longer rings.

Sparrows flock into a tornado
over grazing cattle—
the unconcerned cows
unaware of the slaughterhouse—
lick water from a stream
that feeds the Blue Earth River.

Old grain elevator door and windows
hang lazy as a stalled bucket loader
under the dust and afternoon sun.
Corn and soy commodity prices
rise then recede like lake levels
between spring and fall.

m otis aavenüe

The limestone drive to your farm
hidden under hemp and thistle
beyond the ditch and maple tree line.
I want to mail myself home—
to the house
that no longer lives there.

Exit 102 provides a two-way sign—
two choices to turn
along the state highway
lined with barbed wire fence posts
that establish a half-mile setback
for each hog barn.

No mail today—
it is time to write another letter.

Interstate 90 near Exit 102

Sun sets on pea fields—
June, July—
not hot enough for August.

Sea of Iowa
horizon
south end of Minnesota—

thousands of acres
stacked end-row
on end-row of hay, corn, beans.

Gnats mate near my ear.
Radio
squelches and reports on wind speed,

current direction——
note the time—
twenty hours, three minutes.

A flash of white light—
glyphosate
drifts from overhead—wide tail

suspended behind
crop duster—
until it turns, dusts again.

Pigweed goes to sleep—
green rows
turn spotted brown in two days—

the leaves of weeds dead
or dying
in strict military time.

The seeds live again
next season.
Someone else will fill my space.

Sulfur yellow sky
soon sinks deep
into indigo. The bugs

are all gone except
fireflies.
A canopy of stars shine.

Things I Could Be

If I could be a bubble of sea foam
rising from a galley's ancient belly
sunk in deep shades of primordial waves,
we would band together at the surface
and form a vast continent of white brine.

I would be a groovy record jacket
to your favorite world music album—
all folksy and bluesy and jazzy too.

I might wrap myself in Christmas paper
with tinsel and a bow, hugged in your hands
while you test me with a curious shake—

Lift you through satellite high above clouds
give you a birds-eye view of your planet—
country, state, county, city, apartment.
As a tall communication tower
you could broadcast yourself around the globe
like a short public service announcement.

I would be a seed of your favorite tree—
grow tall and straight and cover you with leaves
as you dangle from my sagging branches.

I would be a thirteen trombone brass band
and flash reflections of your smiling face.

You could breathe me in as misted sea air,
carry me, with you always, in your lungs.

Bird-Watching at the Edge of Town

Sparrows bounce along a concrete slab
in an abandoned sidewalk
and onto the grass
near a patch of Great Plains White Fringed Orchids—
like tiny diplomats—
shoulders back, filling their bloused chests with farm air,
throats forward.
She should be among their kind.

A wife chooses a man—a pigeon—
working ground for kernels of corn,
for crusts of muffin and cake.
If she were a bird, her feathers
would shake off rain.

Flying overhead
in a flocked, twisting, stream—
into the sky of cirrus clouds,
returning toward the earth—
before landing on telephone wire.
She would still love me.

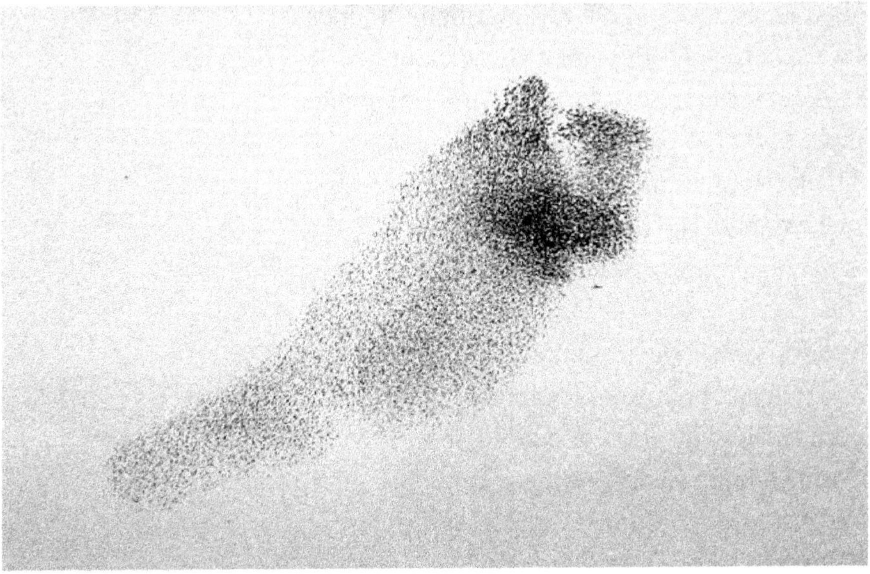

Abandoned Farms and Fields They Own

We talk of Nietzsche and supermen—flames
like supernova—the green wood campfire
smokes away mosquito, gnat, sense of smell,
three nights of backcountry body odor.
Thick siltation of the Blue Earth River
makes removing blindness impossible
to see the walleye wait for easy worms.

We whisper about Bikini Atoll
and neutron bombs and listen for wrist-high
corn rustle with coon or coyote or wind.
Sulfur bombs we buy at the county fair
are perfect for stopping high school finals.
The tiny glass is so easy to crush—
conceal and control simple contraband.

We wonder how old-growth Minnesota
must have looked before telegraph and rail
connected farm towns and lean country folk—
like our families—maybe softer, more plump.
Coonhounds howl around midnight—someone close.

Hotdogs burn over hot coals while we sit
toward the top of our closest oak tree
and wonder again if danger will pass.
Later, burned and blistered, we throw hotdogs
at the weakest member of our party.
He gropes the air, grins, and drops to black earth—
craves attention like a flame consumes fuel—
sometimes stoked with Kodiak Snuff and Schell's
Beer brewed and distributed in New Ulm.

We all try some acting as one person—
one people alone and isolated
regardless—like fireflies sparking yards
into the shallow horizon where soil
meets muddy water and common grasses
grow toothy silhouettes of gray shadow.
The next morning we will all return home.

Pretending Play War

Wheels grind steal laid between box elder trees
dead from beetle attack—losing all leaves
to crimson, jaundice, mandarin—my skull
twelve feet from slowing grain car momentum.

A gray cumulus cloud shades eyes from sun—
this view like cotton T-shirt distilled light—
a diesel train engine drones along its haul
and pops over joints connecting the tracks.

We keep camouflage cover of milkweed.
Grasses snap. I stop breathing last season's
soybeans fermented in puddles of brine
beneath sheet metal elevator shoots.

My chest and train hitch together—thunder
as each pound themselves—double length and load.
His eyes flinch shut. We are under attack.
My friend, fragments in his shallow foxhole.

A mortar blast—his hopeless, hands-off life
ends short by mixing cocktails with his car—
timeless, unending boom in memory.
The faceless threat of paranoid hate crimes—

dialogue of guns report far from here—
from across a red sea of horizon,
old wounds carried to the front through past lives.
Union Pacific whistle drops in pitch

west of town. Danger passes like field fire.
I sit up to realize my certain death—
the opposition entrenched behind us
to claim me as a casualty of war.

If I Were a Song

If I were a song
I would be a little tune
people whistle on their way to the bank
or while they walk to a friend's house
for a slice of apple pie—

perhaps a Christmas carol
sung by a choir
or the background score of a feature film
performed by a symphony orchestra.

Being a march played by a brass band
could be neat
or an electric guitar solo
my dad jams in his garage.

I would not prefer to be a hum
people think of when they have to see the principal
of a school—
or the dentist.

I don't want to be that music
in dentist's lounges
or in elevators either.

Going to the dentist hurts—
for a little while—
but not as much as the toothaches they fix.

Maybe I should be a song on the radio
that people hear in their car
on the way home from the dentist,
and
I could be a song that everybody
sings along with.

Five Degrees below Zero on New Year's Day

Blue Earth River's banks
like a wet Swisher—
the cigar split at its seams.

Blue ice bruised brown—snow
cracks under new snow
as the cold water
springs from a fresh hole.

My clothes smell like bleach.

Wind burns tears from eyes.

Minnows surface—fear
expressed in zigzags—
as the ice sinks slow.

Tiny clear water
lake swallows frozen
water—finally
dry air leaches fish
from their little lives.

Union Pacific
freight train shakes
tarred trestle timbers
overhead—a diesel
engine tugs its load
and high in the sky,
covered by dark clouds,
a faint fingernail
of sun disappears.

Walking Home through Fields of Snow

Rusted Maytag washing machine slug-holed
as a noodle strainer against wood doors
of the grain shed—hung on crippled hinges
like loose teeth. Exhaust from an ethanol
plant scrapes against inversion atmosphere—
as if cotton gobs flooded the fingers
of naked tree pen and ink skeletons.

We could blow up this city without shame—
blow up ourselves with gasoline glass jars.

A squirrel, flat and frozen, near a pile
of red railroad granite bares yellow teeth
behind bent swollen lips. Caprice Classic
—municipal blue—police car prowls
past boot prints pressed in virgin drifted snow.
Nothing of this world seems truthful or real.

Fishing for Carp

With quarter ounce weights
and barbed hooks
like bent harpoons
we catch carp heavy as legs.

Controlling a six-inch blade
cutting chicken liver
in half for bait
to crane fish from the water
seems like a comfort.
Their beer bottle mouths
drown on air—
her prehistory scales
pressed from flakes of smelted gold.
She had her mouth hooked
at least once before.

Her brain must be a pea—
or only a brain stem like a broken strand
of 40-pound test line.
She swallows the leader to her guts
leaving little hope for survival.

Bullheads bite too—
fat and full of field
runoff from spring snow.
Their yellow bellies
stained with red spots.
Soon the soybean
planting will end
and school will let out
leaving us unemployed
for the summer—
until baling hay begins
and we buck it in the barn
for winter.

Reflections of Light in Muddy Water

The Blue Earth River, dark and muddy,
drags our dirt to New Orleans—
Mississippi River Delta rich in nitrogen,
protein and places like Ledyard,
Guckeen, Delavan, Nashville Township—
overcome with the mixing authority of water.

It is too late to bring this clay
and sediment back. Clam shells
litter the sandbar
and the humid air is dense with dead carp
and bullhead laid in the ragweed.
I don't feel like casting a fishing line
today. Sitting half-lotus
I become the fish and feel bottom
for insight that sustains life.

Take refuge in the Trinity,
in the Buddha, in Dharma and Sangha
until attaining enlightenment
and rest free from suffering
and the cause of suffering.
Attain enlightenment
for the benefit of all the little varmints
so we may never be separate from happiness
free of attachment and aversion,
so we may serve our purpose like the river,
like the shells,
like the fish,
like all the little critters
mixing life with life—
an eternal cycle—a triangle
touching all equal sides
until we return to the sea.

If I Were a Dollar

If I were a dollar
I would huddle in a portfolio
of stocks and bonds
so I could grow up one day to be a bigger bill—
like a fifty or one-hundred—
or I could split into one hundred single dollars
of myself like clones
and we could all catch carp on Rice Lake
every summer,
me and the other 99 me.

I would break out from my piggy bank
and make change into different currencies
like a peso,
a rupee,
yen,
euro,
or kwacha
and then purchase pulled taffy
from all the countries and share it with my friends.

If I were part of a low interest loan,
I could help build a duplex,
a Methodist Church,
or a chewing gum factory
that also sells helium balloons
and managed by a large man with a mustache
that reminds me of grandpa.
But if the unfixed rate of interest
went from 5 to 10 to 20,
I would have to go back to the bank's safe
and spend the night in the dark.

If I were a dollar I would be green
and adopt George Washington's face
as my face too—
tape the words In God We Trust to my back.
I would then move to Washington, D.C.
and live in the Federal Treasury
so I should jog with the President of the United States
each morning and visit the U.S. Mint
to make sure all the new bills
look as clean and wrinkle free as I do.

The Distant Shore

A thousand streetlights
on the distant shore
remind me of the Milky Way

and lying on our backs
under all those stars—
it's hard not to feel so small.

My heart's attacked
knowing this too shall pass.
I wish time would wait for me.

Seems like the loose ends
that make our lives
return to nothing eventually.

It's nice to hold you
and keep you warm.
Wind blows cold across the bay.
Staring into the folding waves,
I realize the answer to it all.

Even though waters change
a distant shore will remain
and comfort comes from things we do
for one another.

I have to wake you
from sleeping on the sand.
The moon pulls in the tide

and over our shoulders
as we walk away;
the sun rises through red clouds.

Things We Have Grown to See:

Earwigs, crab cakes, garden gnome,
chocolate, contrails, switchblade combs—
tricycles and ocean foam. Soup
also, matchbooks too; woodchuck, cornstalks—
underpants?

Flashlights and a tiny broken bulb.
          Steering wheel and dashboard dust.
Pineapple diced into cubes—
          Cheddar cheese and chicken's feet.
Floppy disks, bats, or chopping blocks.

Aluminum alloy shopping carts.
Rain clouds rolled like cigarette smoke.
Mullets, staples, talcum powder,
iced tea and soda cans and mayoral candidates.

Toilet paper hung in an old oak tree,
technical writing in Chinese; coffee-stain circles,
ink pens, and calculus equations.

Two boots, one sock like a missing tooth.
The white, full moon radiates earth shine.
Zigzag scribble | creosote-treated railroad tie.

Vanilla ice cream on a cake batter cone
and candy sprinkles plus crushed nuts
with hydrogenated, emulsified, liquid butterscotch
swirled through the center of its lactose galaxy.
A mummified pharaoh existing beyond his natural life—
a word, a sentence, a poem, a book, a binary file
of archived public records. Deeds.

Distilled spirits, beakers, and one periodic table.
Thousands of faces and occasional names.
Newspaper, paste, paper mache—
Pope John Paul II, sometimes on the Internet…

A knee joint, torso, a face reflected in a family photo.

m otis aavenüe

SELECTED POEMS FROM DEVILS TOWER

m otis aavenüe's first chapbook

Geometry of Men and Women

Lightning bugs
blink along rectangle beds of roses.
          Silhouettes of oak
          bathe in moon-bleached shadow.

I deconstruct the conversation
we had between sips of Sumatran coffee
          between subtle glances
          sincere as puppy awe—

my equilateral skull
cocked in acute angle.

Parallel as reflections in water
I felt with you then
          we hugged like conjoined twins
          in the same plaid pajamas—

symmetrical
in point-of-view and unable to part
          from comparing failed love
          to failed love.

m otis aavenüe

People of our pasts
fell like baby teeth from gums—
Euclidean smiles
webbed across faces.

I could have kissed
the perpendicular nap at the base of your nose
the Roman arches
above your eyes.

Instead
I offer to refill your empty cup
and we rotate away
through proved equations.

With Five Ranch Hands Remembering the Klamath

One

Wind blows like cedar
sway between marble valleys.
The rocks sweat water.
        Tenements of moss
        rent rooms to banana slugs
        while the grasses die—
                their blades piss yellow.
                I feel like grass in the sun
                and smile regardless.

With Five Ranch Hands Remembering the Klamath

Two

I picked a flower—
this center of all things—held
it with one finger.
        I could have crushed the stem
        with dull botany tweezers
        and shaking gray hands—
                it was fragile life,
                and along the steep hillside
                thousands covered earth.

With Five Ranch Hands Remembering the Klamath

Three

The half cratered gulch
like a bitten green apple
cups spring's melting snow.
        Our pregnant cattle
        croon for the mountain meadows
        remembered as calves.
                I twist my mustache,
                throw coffee grounds in the dirt—
                this life has been fine.

With Five Ranch Hands Remembering the Klamath

Four

Late spring in Klamath,
when snow runs like Rocky Road
ice cream from mountains,
we'd fist gray granite
to pelt the brown hides of deer
and drive them—grunting,
salt hungry—from camp.
These memories go under my
pillow while I sleep.

With Five Ranch Hands Remembering the Klamath

Five

I watched the brook trout
eye drowning horseflies, intent
on filling bellies,
        before stabbing pool
        with sunburned arms to jerk them
        from concentric rings.
                It was a good meal
                to work for on Sunday nights.
                I'd laugh and give thanks.

Driving through the Ozarks at Night with a Friend Once Thought to Be Dead

Crickets consume the neighborhood
with buzzes loud as transistors.

Behind his rock quarried shoulders
vacant lots of dead grass shift like tide,
and he lifts his steam shovel head,
mastodon slow, to scrape answers
from Springfield's limestone layered cliffs.

Cowlicks of brown bushes and shrub
on red hills wear the smell of skunks.

The night's humid air reminds me
I am six hundred miles from bed
and battle fatigues with no bus
ticket, address, or phone number.

Embedded along the highway
in concrete, all the smooth pebbles
point northward to Minnesota.

m otis aavenüe

The dead face of the moon rises,
rises on tails of falling stars
behind lazy sagging cable
between house and empty white house.

Together we careen over
broken streets, past construction signs
half shadowed as charcoal sketches
in a closing book—his moon face
Jesus hung in the driver's seat—
mine like a hydrogen zeppelin
torpedoed through inches of space
to collide with the lunar cheek.

I turn, eye to eye, with the black
planet of my thin reflection
in the passenger side window.
He states I was as good a friend
as a friend ever expected.

ABOUT THE AUTHOR

No one knows where m otis aavenüe disappeared in the Sonoran Desert or how he may have passed. Only his glass eye remained trapped under a manzanita bush. Family and friends believe he died practicing a lifestyle he loved. Evidence suggests a mountain lion consumed his body. Others have created a legend that while sleeping under the stars, the hated Chupacabra discovered him. Some still speculate he illegally crossed the border into Mexico and continued a path toward Argentina. We may never discover all the facts.

We do know he was hiking across America in search of the raw truth of his life and inspiration for a nonfiction book about combining living in poverty with practicing deep ecology. We also know he left many of his unpublished and unfinished works with his close friend, publisher, and property manager, Matthew Reinders, who continues to be his best advocate and ally.

MicroDot Media is now proud to publish m otis aavenüe's work. Grasses of Nashville Township holds no claim on fictional characters designed to illustrate a narrative arc unlike his first chapbook, Devils Tower. This collection of landscape poems, song lyrics, and poems for children is the voice of the author. Grasses of Nashville Township offers a peek into the relationship between the observer and the observed at the places where rivers meet their oceans.

We have worked diligently to preserve m otis aavenüe's original formats; however, we have also taken liberty to edit and produce his craft of the written word so his restless and free spirit may live on.

Thank You.

Find more online:

www.microdotbooks.com

To contact friends of m otis aavenüe email otis.aavenue@gmail.com

Look for these other great books by m otis aavenüe

1. Devils Tower

www.ingramcontent.com/pod-product-compliance
Lightning Source LLC
Chambersburg PA
CBHW071646040426
42452CB00009B/1781
9780984855308